Here's a passport to adventure
to a lover of adventure
BRIAN, Happy Birthday!
Hope you'll visit these
May 6, 1993 places!
Robin Rector Krupp

Let's Go Traveling

BY AIR MAIL
PAR AVION

FIVE YEAR DIARY

PASSPORT

Bon Voyage
Rachel—
Have a
wonderful trip!

RACHEL'S
Scrapbook

THERE IS A THRILLING TIME
AHEAD FOR YOU

YOU WILL VISIT SOME FARAWAY LAND THAT HAS LONG BEEN IN YOUR WAKING THOUGHTS.

Let's Go Traveling

Written and illustrated by
Robin Rector Krupp

Morrow Junior Books
New York

For all my art teachers, especially
Donald Lent,
Mac McCloud,
Barbara Bottner,
Richard Milholland,
and Sharon Kagan

Photographic and artistic acknowledgments: Editions du Castelet, 13; Editions d'art Yvon, 13; Editions René, 14, 15; Crown Copyright, 16, 17; Alan Sorrell, 16, 17; John Kenney, 16, 17; West Air Photography, The Airport, Weston-super-Mare, England, 18, 19; Ethan H. Krupp, 20, 32, 36; Lehnert and Landrock, 20; Harry Burton, Metropolitan Museum of Art, 22; Lee Boltin, 23, 30; Dover Publications, Inc., 24, 33, 36; Frank Goodman, 25; Sam Waagenaar, 25; China Travel and Tourism Press, 26; Huang Taopeng, Li Miao, China Pictorial, 26, 27; Leo Hilber, 26, 27; J. Kipi Turok, 28; William M. Ferguson, 29; H. Steirlin, 29; Sougez, 29; Walter Dräyer, 30; Walter R. Aguiar, 31; Linda Shele, Mary Miller, 31; Turistica Peninsular Fitzmacolor, 31; Kunstraum München E.V., 32, 33; E. C. Krupp, 33, 36; Foto Corbacho, 33; Maria Reiche, 33; Jian Chen, 33; Javier Ferran, 33; Linda Houghton, 34; Edward Ranney, 34, 35; Photo Precision Limited, 37; Alain Roussot, 38, 39. Technical assistance: Susanna Butsch, Meredith Charpentier, Bian Depei, E. C. Krupp, Eleanor Sapadin Mason, Abbas Nadim, Nicholas Pattengale, Jody Stefansson, Gary Urton, Zhang Ze-min.

Copyright © 1992 by Robin Rector Krupp

Printed in Singapore at Tien Wah Press.
1 2 3 4 5 6 7 8 9 10

Library of Congress Cataloging-in-Publication Data
Krupp, Robin Rector.
Let's go traveling / written and illustrated by Robin Rector
Krupp.
p. cm.
Summary: Presents a trip to the prehistoric caves of France, the pyramids of Egypt, the Maya temples of Mexico, and other ancient wonders of the world.
ISBN 0-688-08989-5. —ISBN 0-688-08990-9 (lib. bdg.)
1. Travel—Juvenile literature.   2. Voyages and travels—Juvenile literature.   [1. Travel. 2. Voyages and travels.   3. Civilization, Ancient.] I. Title.
G175.K78 1992
910.4—dc20   91-21845   CIP   AC

I'd like to go traveling
to the ancient world. I
want to see what's left
of our mysterious past.

TIMELINE

—14,000 B.C.—

PALEOLITHIC PERIOD IN FRANCE,
500,000 B.C. TO 10,000 B.C.

—13,000 B.C.—

ROUFFIGNAC
IN FRANCE,
13,000 B.C.

—12,000 B.C.—

—11,000 B.C.—

B.C.—*abbreviation
for before Christ*

—10,000 B.C.—

— 9000 B.C.—

— 8000 B.C.—

— 7000 B.C.—

— 6000 B.C.—

— 5000 B.C.—

— 4000 B.C.—

NEOLITHIC PERIOD
IN ENGLAND,
3700 B.C. TO 2000 B.C.

— 3000 B.C.—

GREAT PYRAMID
IN EGYPT,
2550 B.C. TO 2530 B.C.

STONEHENGE
IN ENGLAND,
3000 B.C. TO 2000 B.C.

— 2000 B.C.—

TUTANKHAMUN, KING
OF EGYPT,
1334 B.C. TO 1325 B.C.

AVEBURY
IN ENGLAND,
2500 B.C. TO 2200 B.C.

— 1000 B.C.—

GREAT WALL
OF CHINA,
220 B.C. TO A.D. 1644

EMPEROR QIN OF CHINA,
BORN 259 B.C., DIED 210 B.C.

—0—

CLASSIC MAYA IN MEXICO,
A.D. 350 TO A.D. 800

CLASSIC NASCA IN PERU,
400 B.C. TO A.D. 600

— A.D. 1000—

CLASSIC INCA IN PERU,
A.D. 1100 TO A.D. 1535

TUTANKHAMUN'S TOMB
DISCOVERED IN EGYPT, 1922

EMPEROR QIN'S BURIED ARMY
DISCOVERED IN CHINA, 1974

— A.D. 2000—

A.D.—*abbreviation
for anno Domini, Latin
for "in the year of the
Lord"; from 20 B.C. to
A.D. 50 is 70 years.*

Here is a list of places and things I want to see. The list goes on forever, but I'd like to start with these:
the prehistoric caves of France,
the standing stones of England,

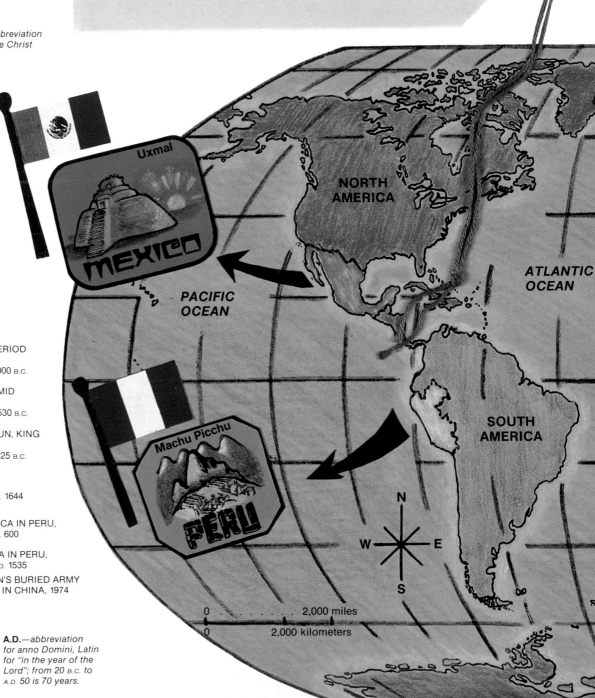

the pyramids of Egypt,
the Great Wall of China,
the Maya temples of Mexico,
the Nazca lines and Inca cities of Peru.
Are these places really out there?
Come along and see!

We'll begin with France and its prehistoric caves, filled with paintings and carvings from long ago.

I'd like to leave tomorrow, but we have to plan. We need travel information, and there's lots of it around. Let's try libraries and bookstores, travel agencies, newspapers, even magazines.

Look at all our choices! I love the chance to choose. Each trip will be special, quite different from the rest.

FRANCE

France is located in western Europe.
Capital: Paris
Official language: French
Official name: République Francaise
Money: 100 centimes = 1 franc
Area: 220,668 square miles
Helpful phrases:
Hello: *bon jour*
Please: *s'il vous plait*
Thank you: *merci*
Good-bye: *au revoir*

ENGLAND

England is part of an island nation in northwestern Europe.
Capital: London
Official name: England, part of Great Britain and the United Kingdom
Official language: English
Area: 50,327 square miles
Money: 100 new pence = 1 pound sterling
Helpful phrases:
Hello: hello, good day
Please: please
Thank you: thank you
Good-bye: good-bye, cheerio

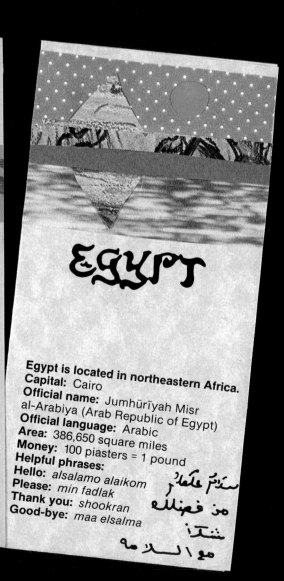

EGYPT

Egypt is located in northeastern Africa.
Capital: Cairo
Official name: Jumhūrīyah Misr al-Arabiya (Arab Republic of Egypt)
Official language: Arabic
Area: 386,650 square miles
Money: 100 piasters = 1 pound
Helpful phrases:
Hello: *alsalamo alaikom*
Please: *min fadlak*
Thank you: *shookran*
Good-bye: *maa elsalma*

السلام عليكم
من فضلك
شكرا
مع السلامة

☺ You will step on the soil of many countries. ☺

Travel with few expectations and a happy heart.

One serious thing to know: Nothing is to be taken too seriously.

CHINA

China is located in eastern and central Asia.
Capital: Beijing
Official name: Zhonghua Renmin Gonghe Guo (People's Republic of China)
Official language: Mandarin Chinese
Area: 3,705,390 square miles
Money: 100 fen = 1 yuan
Helpful phrases:
Hello: *ni hao*
Please: *ching*
Thank you: *xie xie*
Good-bye: *zai jian*

你好 請 謝謝 再見

MEXICO

Mexico is located in the southern part of North America.
Capital: Mexico City
Official name: Estado Unidos Mexicanos (United Mexican States)
Official language: Spanish
Area: 761,604 square miles
Money: 100 centavos = 1 peso
Helpful phrases:
Hello: *buenos días*
Please: *por favor*
Thank you: *gracias*
Good-bye: *adiós*

PERU

Peru is located on the west coast of South America.
Capital: Lima
Official name: República del Peru (Republic of Peru)
Official languages: Spanish and Quechua
Area: 496,222 square miles
Money: 100 centimos = 1 inti
Helpful phrases:

	Spanish	**Quechua**
Hello:	*buenos días*	*allillanchu*
Please:	*por favor*	*yusulpayki*
Thank you:	*gracias*	*añaychayki*
Good-bye:	*adiós*	*allinllaña*

We decide to go in summer. We'll fly to Paris, then take a train. It will be fun to camp and join a local tour. There are so many details to remember; we write lots and lots of lists. We're glad we saved our money. Tickets, meals, admissions—our expenses will add up.

TRAVEL TIPS

Cave of Pech Merle at Cabrerets (46). Prehistoric drawings (50 painted, 10 engraved), in a remarkable natural décor. Cirques (natural...

Betharram (64). A mile and a half of caves which amateur speleologists may explore without difficulty in 1 1/2 hours. The underground river can be sailed on. La Medous (65). Traces of a prehistoric settlement. Bear and hyena bones.

Hope for the best, but prepare for the worst.

Packing List
Hat
Rain hat
Rain coat
Boots
Socks
underwear
3 pairs pants
5 shirts
1 warm sweater
1 warm jacket
1 skirt with pockets
1 vest with pockets
walking shoes
1 dress (cotton with pockets)
½ slip
pajamas
extra shoes!

things
Backpack
tent
sleeping bag
ground cloth
stakes
address book
maps
little Bible
pencils (colored)
sketchbook
camera
guide books

TWENTY U.S. DOLLARS

el Rose
64 916 940
20

Please send me more information.
Name: RACHEL ROSE
Address:
City:
State: Zip:

FRANCE
FRENCH GOVERNMENT TOURIST OFFICE

CYCLING TRIPS
FREE CATALOG
BIKE TOURS ABROAD

SADIE

TO RACHEL
GOOD LUCK
BYE
FROM YOUR BEST FRIEND, SARAH

Bring home some souvenirs

I close my eyes and imagine that I'm on a trip. What am I wearing? I'll pack whatever I imagine!

Valentine the Wonder Dog

Return travel books to library
TRIP FRANCE

Friday Morning
Dear Rachel,
I'll miss you while you are gone. How about some souvenirs we could share? On your trip you could collect
• Post Cards • Coins
• Business Cards • Stamps
• Bottle Caps • Small Rocks
• Shells • Matchbook Covers
• Feathers • Used tickets
Whatever you do, have fun.
Love and Kisses
Grandpa Robert

We're excited and nervous, wondering what to expect. The travel agent says, "Expect the unexpected. Plans always change, and some things can go wrong. You'll find languages and customs different from our own."

But we're ready for all kinds of adventures. Kiss everyone good-bye!

Fix wheel on suitcase

check airport reservations

Ask neighbors pets

Paris

FRANCE

$20 UNITED STATES

Dear Diary,
We leave in 16 days
This is our first trip together. We'll be in France for three weeks. By then I will have written a lot. I'm curious. What will happen?

Dear Diary,
We leave in 9 days, 10 hours and 22 days minutes (I'm counting!)
I got my passport today. It's a little book with my name and photograph. (My photo looks terrible!) As I enter and leave each country, the customs officer will stamp my passport with the date and place. That way, they can keep track of the people who visit their country.

Dear Diary,
We leave in 6 hours and 3 minutes (still counting!)
Today I took my money to the bank and got traveler's checks. If they are lost or stolen, they can be replaced. I had to sign each one! We leave tomorrow!

Dear Diary,
We leave in 5 days,
I'm a little worried. Will I have enough money? Am I packing too much? Maybe I've forgotten something. And my pets—will they be okay?
P.S. I promised my teacher I'd keep a list of new words and their definitions. Oh goody. When I get home Dad will type it for me.
P.S.S. I'm almost PACKED!

Getting there isn't easy. We wait in lines and go through airport security. Then we take a long flight. The plane is crowded and it's hard to sleep. But everything is worth it because we're here in **France**!

Each day we visit one or two prehistoric caves. We stay in groups with French-speaking guides. They point out animals that were carved or painted on cave walls at least 15,000 years ago.

Dear Diary,
I think I've got jet lag. The clock says it's morning. My body says it's the middle of the night! I'm REALLY HERE!

☼ ☽ ⊕ :zzzzzz

P.S. French fries ~~here~~ are called pommes frites here.
P.S.S. Lascaux, the most famous cave, was found by 4 boys and their dog named Pilot.

Dear Diary,
We all have to be careful in the caves. I couldn't wear my backpack because it might scrape the art. Lights, flashlights, even our warm breath can be harmful. The guides turn the lights off as we leave each section. If a cave gets too fragile, they have to close it to the public.

Paris, France

Les Eyzies, France

Pech-Merle cave,
20,000 B.C. to 15,000 B.C.

Sometimes the animals are hard to see, and we really have to look. Sometimes they are life-size and looming over us.

We are quiet, knowing that prehistoric people stood here such a long time ago. They lived in rock shelters and wore animal skins. Did they think their art was magic? Was it a prayer that would help them with their hunt? It feels like a mystery story wrapped up in a fairy tale.

My New Word List

extinct—no longer existing
paleolithic—from the earliest part of the Stone Age. Paleolithic tools were chipped out of stone. In France, the paleolithic period lasted from about 500,000 B.C. to 10,000 B.C.
prehistoric—"before history," meaning before writing was invented
stalactite—a formation of limestone rock that hangs like an icicle from the ceiling of a cave
stalagmite—a formation of limestone rock that is built up like a cone from the floor of a cave

Each cave is special and hard to describe. My favorite is "The Cave of 100 Mammoths," called Rouffignac (pronounced *roofing yak*). This cave is so gigantic, we ride an electric train one mile inside!

We're amazed to learn that cave bears lived here long ago. We pass dirt mounds hollowed out for their hibernation nests. We pass scratchings where they sharpened up their claws.

GROTTE DE ROUFFIGNAC - DORDOGNE

Then we see paintings of horses, ibex, woolly rhinoceroses, and woolly mammoths. The paint has lasted for over 15,000 years. But now some of these animals are extinct. Imagine meeting this bear deep inside a cave!

There's more to tell, but let's go on to the next trip. We'll move ahead in history about 10,000 years.

Huge stones could have been moved with logrollers.

STONEHENGE

SCOTLAND

NORTH SEA

United Kingdom

NORTHERN IRELAND

IRISH SEA

ENGLAND

N

REPUBLIC OF IRELAND

WALES

AVEBURY

ATLANTIC OCEAN

LONDON

STONEHENGE

ENGLISH CHANNEL

FRANCE

Stonehenge as it might have appeared in the final phase of its construction, about 1550 B.C.

Stonehenge, looking west

Now we're in **England** to see the giant standing stones. Stonehenge, a famous circle, stands alone on Salisbury Plain. It looks like it is waiting there, waiting just for us.

We read the guidebook and listen to the guards. Seeing the real thing helps the facts sink in. It is older, taller, larger than I thought.

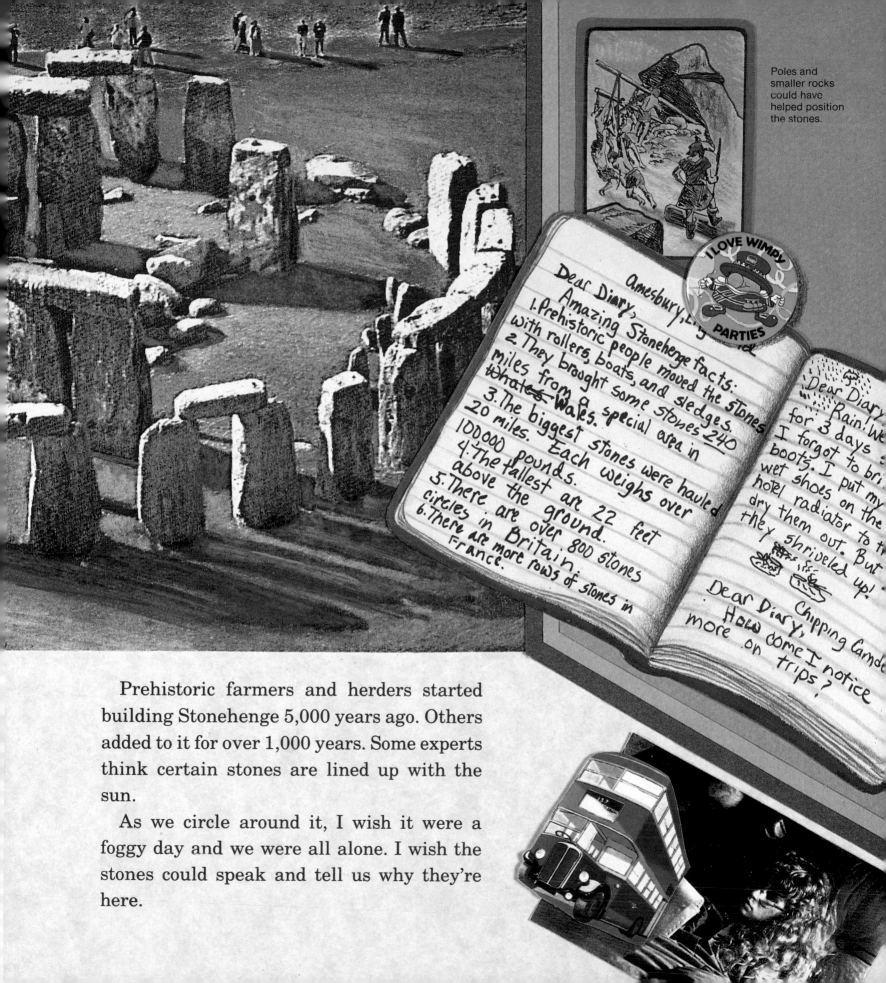

Poles and smaller rocks could have helped position the stones.

Amesbury, England

Dear Diary,
Amazing Stonehenge facts:
1. Prehistoric people moved the stones with rollers, boats, and sledges.
2. They brought some stones 240 miles from a special area in Wales.
3. The biggest stones were hauled 20 miles. Each weighs over 100000 pounds.
4. The tallest are 22 feet above the ground.
5. There are over 800 stones circles in Britain.
6. There are more rows of stones in France.

Dear Diary,
Rain! We ___ for 3 days. I forgot to bri___ boots. I put my wet shoes on the hotel radiator to t___ dry them out. But they shriveled up!

Chipping Camde___

Dear Diary,
How come I notice more on trips?

Prehistoric farmers and herders started building Stonehenge 5,000 years ago. Others added to it for over 1,000 years. Some experts think certain stones are lined up with the sun.

As we circle around it, I wish it were a foggy day and we were all alone. I wish the stones could speak and tell us why they're here.

Avebury as it might have appeared in 2200 B.C., looking north

archaeology—the scientific study of the people, customs, and life of ancient times

two lines of stones named The Avenue

original entrance

remaining stones of the South Circle

original entrance

remaining stones of the Central Circle

original entrance

Avebury, looking south

Amesbury, England

Dear Sarah,

We've been staying in hotels and little inns. Last night we stayed with an English family in their home. We paid to spend the night in their extra bed-room. In the morning we had a delicious break-fast. There was a sign out front that said: BED AND BREAKFAST. I met their son named Miles. We're going to be pen pals and start collecting stamps. I miss you.

Your pal, RACHEL

The next day we visit Avebury (*aev-berry*). People built a giant circle of earth here over 4,000 years ago. Its purpose isn't known. But it is so large that now there's a town built right inside!

We start at the museum and learn what there is to see. There are lots more standing stones, a giant hill of earth, and a long earth-covered tomb.

West Kennet Long Barrow

Silbury Hill

Great Britain—
an island made up of England, Scotland, and Wales

megalith—
a big stone

Neolithic—
from the last part of the Stone Age, marked by the beginning of farming and the use of polished stone tools. In England, the Neolithic period lasted from 3700 B.C. to 2000 B.C.

trilithon—
a prehistoric archway formed by two big, upright stones and one big stone across their top

United Kingdom—
a kingdom made up of Great Britain and Northern Ireland

They all seem mysterious. So much knowledge has been lost. But archaeologists discover new things about old places all the time.

Now let's go hiking and see everything up close. I love so much exploring, especially when there's a picnic lunch. What's over that next hill? One discovery leads to another. Let's go on for more!

Stow-on-the-Wold, England
Dear Grams and Gramps,
This afternoon we stopped for tea. The waiter brought around a cart called the trolley. It had sweeties, crumpets, tarts, and scones. We crammed ourselves with sweets.
Love, Rachel
P.S. People drive on the wrong side of the street here!
Oink!Oink!

REMEMBER to use the POST CODE!

Avebury, Wiltshire
South-western sector of ditch and outer circle
View looking north

the pyramid of Menkaure (also known as Mycerinus), who ruled from 2532 B.C. to 2504 B.C.; the grandson of Khufu

the pyramid of Khafre (also known as Chephren), who ruled from 2558 B.C. to 2532 B.C.; the son of Khufu

Great Pyramid, or the pyramid of Khufu (Greek, Cheops), who ruled from 2589 B.C. to 2566 B.C.

the Buried Boat

capstone

interior view of the Great Pyramid

481 feet tall

hieroglyph—a picture or symbol used in ancient writing for a word, idea, or sound
Pharaoh—an ancient Egyptian ruler
sphinx—an imaginary creature with the body of a lion and the head of a man, ram, or hawk. There are many sphinx statues in Egypt.

the Sphinx

shaft

shaft

core blocks

packing blocks

casing blocks

King's Chamber

Grand Gallery

Ascending Corridor

Queen's Chamber

escape shaft

Descending Corridor

unfinished chamber

EGYPT

Giza, Egypt
Egyptian men wear long, flowing robes and women carry loads right on their heads!
My name in hieroglyphs
RACHEL
mouth eagle Pool Feather lion

Cairo, Egypt
Dear Diary,
I stare out the window on our tour bus. Today I saw a man sitting at an outdoor cafe. He raised his coffee cup and said "Welcome." I couldn't hear him, but I could read his lips. He said "Welcome." He said it right to me.

Central Bank of Egypt
20

sculpture of Khafre, protected by the falcon god Horus

pyramids and the Sphinx at a Sound and Light show

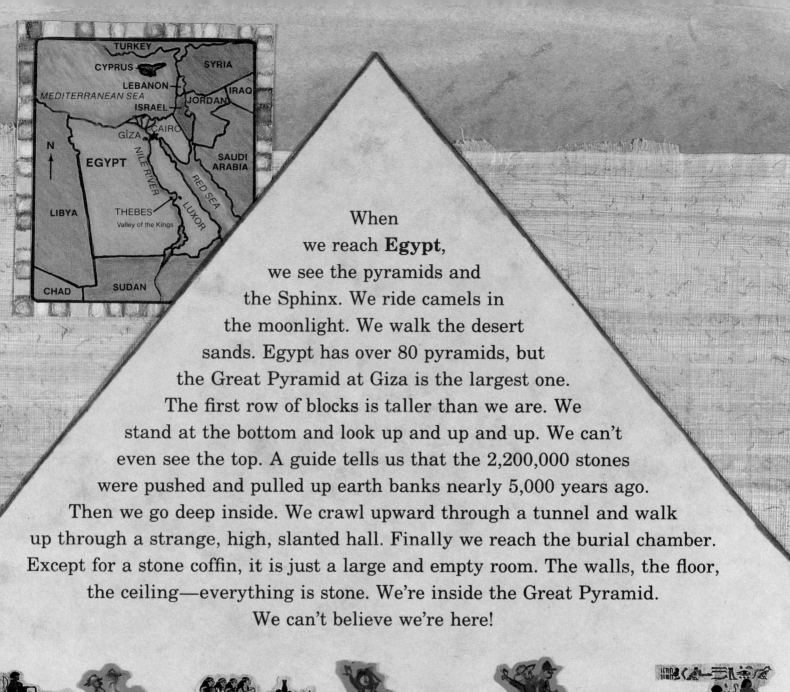

When
we reach **Egypt**,
we see the pyramids and
the Sphinx. We ride camels in
the moonlight. We walk the desert
sands. Egypt has over 80 pyramids, but
the Great Pyramid at Giza is the largest one.
The first row of blocks is taller than we are. We
stand at the bottom and look up and up and up. We can't
even see the top. A guide tells us that the 2,200,000 stones
were pushed and pulled up earth banks nearly 5,000 years ago.
Then we go deep inside. We crawl upward through a tunnel and walk
up through a strange, high, slanted hall. Finally we reach the burial chamber.
Except for a stone coffin, it is just a large and empty room. The walls, the floor,
the ceiling—everything is stone. We're inside the Great Pyramid.
We can't believe we're here!

Howard Carter and his sponsor, Lord Carnavon

the 16 steps leading from the tomb

Tutankhamun's official seal, or cartouche

alabaster stone lion vase found in the tomb

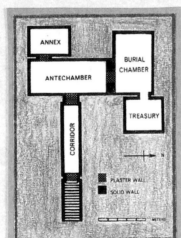

ANNEX

BURIAL CHAMBER

ANTECHAMBER

CORRIDOR

TREASURY

N

PLASTER WALL
SOLID WALL

METERS

first view inside the tomb, looking down the cleared corridor

Tutankhamun's mummy

Valley of the Kings, with Tutankhamun's tomb in front

the clay seal of the House of the Dead

Opposite page: one of the four miniature coffins that contained Tutankhamun's internal organs

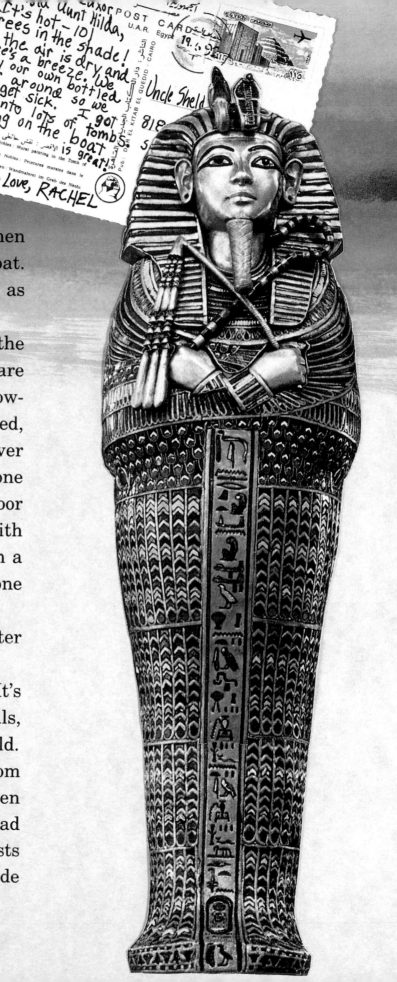

We sail up the Nile from Luxor and then
down again, spending nights aboard a boat.
We wave to all the kids shouting "Hello" as
they run along the shore.

On the West Bank, in the Valley of the
Kings, we pretend the year is 1922. We are
working with an archaeologist named Howard Carter. For six long years we've searched,
sweating in the sun. But today we discover
a very special tomb. First we uncover one
step, then 15 more. We pass through a door
and quickly clear a corridor blocked with
stones. Look, another door, complete with a
seal! This means that for 3,000 years no one
has been inside.

"Can you see anything?" we ask Mr. Carter
as he peers in through a hole.

"Yes, wonderful things!" he answers. It's
full of jumbled treasures—strange animals,
statues, gold—everywhere the glint of gold.

The tomb belongs to Tutankhamun, from
1350 B.C. He was only nine years old when
he became the pharaoh. But by 19, he had
died. No one knows just why. Now he rests
here as a mummy, inside four coffins made
of gold.

the Great Wall

When we go to **China**, we climb along the Great Wall. We start out running, but soon we huff and puff. It's much steeper than we thought! The wall was built to keep out invaders, more than 2,000 years ago.

We meet some Chinese children who become our friends. They know a lot about their country and want to talk with us. They say the Great Wall was started by Emperor Qin (*chin*). Over 1,000,000 people struggled ten years to get part of it built.

China's first emperor was Qin Shi Huang (259 B.C. to 210 B.C.)

Beijing, China

Dear Diary,
I really liked the Great Wall. I'd like to walk the whole length, 3,930 miles. How long would that take?
P.S. Balloons, kites, dominoes, playing cards, and yo-yo's were all invented by the Chinese.

We have about NO seconds to be friends.
1 2 3 4 5 6 7 8 9 10 byee!
Dear Diary,
I learned that if everyone in the world lined up, one out of every four would be Chinese!
In the morning we exercise with other people right on the street. They look graceful doing TAI CHI. We all laugh. I feel like I know them.

Xian, China
Dear Diary,
I love Chinese Trains.
I wave to everyone.

中国龙

UNION OF SOVIET SOCIALIST REPUBLICS
(Soviet Union)

N

MONGOLIA

NORTH KOREA

SOUTH KOREA

INNER MONGOLIA

PAKISTAN

THE GREAT WALL

BEIJING

YELLOW SEA

TIBET

CHINA

XIAN BURIED ARMY

EAST CHINA SEA

BHUTAN

NEPAL

LAOS

TAIWAN

INDIA

HONG KONG

BANGLADESH

BURMA

VIETNAM

SOUTH CHINA SEA

Emperor Qin also had over 7,000 life-size soldiers made out of clay and 400 more made of bronze. This army was buried to guard his tomb. The Chinese have protected these soldiers within a building as big as a football field. When I see how many there are, I am really shocked!

Down the road, we see Qin's tomb. No one knows what is inside. Someday archaeologists will excavate it and we'll all find out. Old writings say the ancient Chinese made a model of their world inside that tomb. It's supposed to have rivers made of mercury and mountains made of jade and pearls and gold.

Emperor Qin's Buried Army is inside this building. His tomb is inside the middle hill in the distance.

bronze—a hard, strong mixture of copper, tin, and other metals
calligraphy—the art of elegant handwriting
dynasty—a line of rulers who are all part of the same family
excavate—to dig out carefully

Xian, China

Dear Valentine the Wonder Dog and Sadie the Cat, I saw pandas at the zoo. They're as cute as you! Now I'm a chopstick expert. I eat rice and drink orange soda pop. I really like Chinese music! I bought some tapes. I'll play them for you. Be good!
LOVE, RACHEL

Valent 5208 Ea Ca

the Pyramid of the Magician

Now we set off for **Mexico** to see what the ancient Maya built 1,300 years ago. We see white limestone buildings baking in the sun.

My favorites are the pyramids with temples on the top. "The Pyramid of the Magician" at Uxmal (*oosh-moll*) is the scariest one. We climb the narrow steps right to the very top. Here we like looking out but not looking down! We can't even see the steps until we get to the very edge. My stomach is in my throat. I'm trying to be brave. I climb down backward, holding on to the chain.

Chac, the long-nosed rain god

looking east, a view of The Pyramid of the Magician and the four-sided building called the Nunnery

Maya—an ancient people of Central America and Mexico. Classic Maya culture flourished from about A.D. 350 to A.D. 800. The ancient Maya were especially advanced in mathematics, astronomy, art, and architecture.

THE UNITED STATES

N

GULF OF CALIFORNIA

MEXICO

GULF OF MEXICO

CHICHÉN ITZÁ

CUBA

MEXICO CITY **UXMAL**

PACIFIC OCEAN

BELIZE

HONDURAS

GUATEMALA

NICARAGUA

EL SALVADOR

PANAMA

COSTA RICA

We travel to another Maya center called Chichén Itzá (*chi-chen eet-za*). We discover the Ball Court and its Temple of the Jaguars, which has columns made of snakes. We pretend to be fierce warriors playing a special game with a rubber ball.

There are stone rings left on the wall, but no one is sure how they were used. We notice details we might have missed before. On carved murals, we see ball players who have their heads chopped off. Now we wonder why. Another tourist tells us most experts think the loser was sacrificed after this mysterious game.

the Great Ball Court

a ball court mural

the Castillo

the Caracol and, in the distance, the Castillo

I want to come back at the equinox to see the → Serpent of Light. Lots of other people come too!

They found it at the airport!

equinox—the times of the year in March and September when the sun rises due east and sets due west. The hours of daylight then equal the hours of night.

Our last trip is to South America to visit the country of **Peru**. We fly over the Nazca desert and look at ancient drawings spread across the plain. We see a monkey, a spider, a hummingbird, and many long, straight lines. Can you tell what each shape is? Sometimes even the experts have to guess.

Our guide is wonderful, one of the best. She makes everything more interesting. She tells us the prehistoric Indians were drawing on the rocky desert for more than 1,700 years. To make the lines, people removed small stones to reveal the ground's lighter color underneath.

Indians held ceremonies on some of the lines. They thought the drawings might help bring mountain water to a land where it never, ever rained.

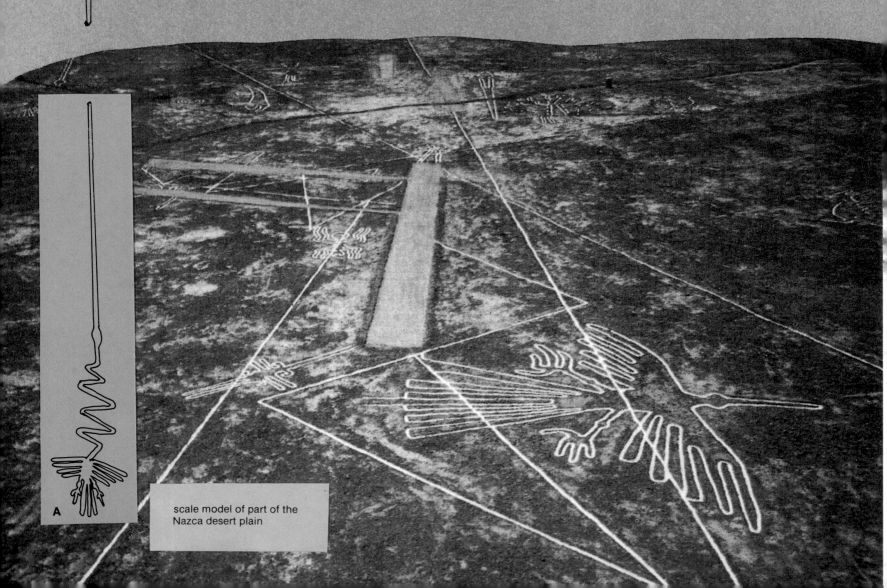

scale model of part of the Nazca desert plain

H I J

Milky Way—the faint band of light stretching across the night sky and composed of millions of distant stars. These stars are part of the Milky Way galaxy. Our solar system is also part of the Milky Way galaxy.

Nasca—an ancient people of southwestern Peru. Classic Nasca culture flourished from about 400 B.C. to A.D. 600. It is known for its many-colored pottery, land irrigation, and giant ground drawings.

Nazca—a town near the giant ground drawings

Identification of the Nazca drawings: **A.** cormorant **B.** lizard **C.** monkey **D.** pelican or frigate bird? **E.** upside–down bat **F.** hummingbird **G.** bird? **H.** yarn? **I.** spider **J.** condor

the orca, or killer whale

Cerámica Nazca

the monkey and surrounding tire tracks

VENEZUELA
PANAMA
COLOMBIA
ECUADOR
AMAZON
N
PERU
BRAZIL
ANDES MOUNTAINS
LIMA ★ MACHU PICCHU
CUZCO
NAZCA
BOLIVIA
PACIFIC OCEAN
CHILE

Dear Folks,
Our tour group is like a big family now. I have a good friend, Ethan. We went to the museum and saw 1500 year old dolls and feather capes and BIG ceramic pots. Last night we went stargazing. I saw the Southern Cross constellation for the first time. The Milky Way looked beautiful—like a night white rainbow.
LOVE, RACHEL
P.S. Peru has mummies too!
P.S.S. This trip I'm collecting feathers.

ICA, Peru

Grandpa Robert
Grandma Margaret
10700 Stradot
Los An

PERU 80

Inti Huatana, or "The Hitching Post of the Sun," approached from the south

Inca—an ancient people of the Cuzco valley in Peru. The Inca empire lasted from about A.D. 1100 to A.D. 1535, when it was conquered by Spain. The Incas are best known for their fine stone buildings, gold, and roads.

Tome
INCA KOLA

12-sided stone in a wall in Cuzco

Cuzco, Peru
Dear Uncle Bruce, aunt Paula, Blake and Clark,
My head really hurt when the plane landed at Cuzco. I had to get used to the altitude. It is 11,000 feet above sea level!
We took the train to Machu Picchu. WOW! I loved it. When we left Machu Picchu, a Peruvian boy raced our bus to the train station. He went straight down the mountain. We zigzagged on hairpin turns. Guess what? The boy won! We gave him some money. Then he had to climb all the way back up! Love and kisses,
RACHEL-THE-TIRED

In Peru, we also see Inca cities from 600 years ago. The Incas were great builders. They used huge, carefully fitted stones.

We visit Machu Picchu (*ma-choo pea-choo*). It's a city of steps. Perched on top of the Andes mountains, it's a picture-postcard spot. We discover hiding places and a secret room. Look! There's a llama grazing, munching on the grass.

We climb up to see the strangely sculptured rock. It's called "The Hitching Post of the Sun." Some say it is a sundial, but no one really knows. By now we're real travel detectives. We like each mystery and want to find out more. But this trip, like the others, is coming to an end.

Machu Picchu

Mary had a little llama.
Mary put it in the zoo.
This was nice for Mary's
mama, comma,
And for me and you!

I wish I knew
who wrote
this!

← Cuzco, Peru

Dear Diary,
When we go back home we'll
have to go through customs
again at the airport. We aren't
allowed to bring in anything
from endangered species
like tortoise shell jewelry
or anything illegal

Machu Picchu,
Peru

Dear Diary,
Today I heard a flute
off in the distance-playing
a Peruvian song. I feel
sort of restless. I want
to stay, but I miss home.

The flight is long, coming from Peru. I feel the same after each trip: lucky to have traveled and thankful to be home. We hug our families and our friends. Even our pets remember us!

Everything has changed. Our world is bigger now. You and I are special friends because we shared the trips. We're full of our adventures and want to tell them all. Yet it's strange that we each liked different parts. The more we tell about what went wrong, the funnier it gets.

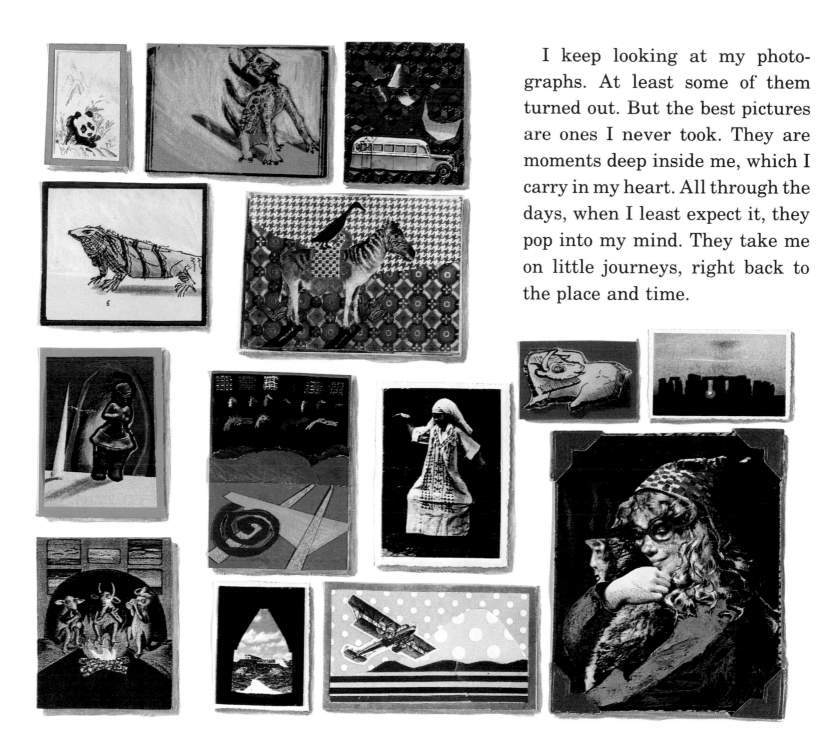

I keep looking at my photographs. At least some of them turned out. But the best pictures are ones I never took. They are moments deep inside me, which I carry in my heart. All through the days, when I least expect it, they pop into my mind. They take me on little journeys, right back to the place and time.

I feel a part of this whole world. I'm amazed at our ancestors and all they did. I understand them better because I walked their lands.

☺ Sing and rejoice, fortune is smiling on you. ☺

It feels good to know that those places are really out there. They really do exist, even when I'm home, even when I sleep.

When the travel dust begins to settle . . .

. . . I begin again to plan. I learn about new places and add them to my list. I'd like to keep on traveling. How about you?

Crete
GREECE

Konarak
India

'Ksan
CANADA

CHILE
Easter Island

Mesa Verde
UNITED STATES

Nemrut Dag
TURKEY